# TOTNES CASTLE

DEVON

❖

## Stewart Brown

*Totnes Castle was built soon after the Norman Conquest in order to control the Saxon town of Totnes and its ancient river crossing over the River Dart. The castle occupies a high, commanding position overlooking the town. Its builder was almost certainly Juhel, one of William the Conqueror's commanders in the Norman campaign which swept through the South-West in 1068. In return for his military service, Juhel was granted Totnes and extensive estates in South Devon.*

*The original eleventh-century castle was an earthwork and timber construction (known today as a 'motte-and-bailey'). The impressive Norman earthworks still survive, comprising a massive earth mound (the 'motte'), and an enclosure at the foot of the motte (the 'bailey'), each surrounded by a deep defensive ditch. The Norman timber defences were later replaced in stone. The stone shell keep crowning the mound was first built in the early thirteenth century, but it was extensively, if not entirely, rebuilt in the late thirteenth or early fourteenth century, much as it survives today. This illustrated handbook provides a guide for visitors to the castle remains, followed by a brief history which tells the broader story of Totnes Castle and town.*

# ❖ CONTENTS ❖

*Published by English Heritage*
*1 Waterhouse Square, 138-142 Holborn, London EC1N 2ST*
*© English Heritage 1998*
*First published by English Heritage 1998*
*Reprinted 2000, 2002, 2006, 2009, 2011*

*Photographs by English Heritage Photographic Unit*
*and copyright of English Heritage, unless otherwise stated.*

*Edited by Lorimer Poultney*
*Designed by Pauline Hull*
*Printed in England by Pureprint Group*
*C30, 5/11, 05830, ISBN 978-1-85074-672-0*

# INTRODUCTION

❖

THE NORMANS introduced the first castles into England, although a few had been built shortly before the actual Conquest of 1066 by Norman followers of King Edward the Confessor. Most parts of the country, however, had not seen any castles before William the Conqueror and his supporters built castles in large numbers throughout his newly-won kingdom.

Norman castles were both offensive and defensive. They were fortified military bases from which mounted

*'Totnes on the River Dart', by J M W Turner, c.1824*

knights could control the surrounding countryside, but they were also strongholds which provided secure accommodation for the new Norman lords to whom William had handed out the property of dispossessed Saxon landholders. In return, the lords promised loyalty, and maintained sufficient forces to keep order.

Castles were constructed in various forms and of various materials, some using stone where this was readily available. The majority, however, were built of timber, since this was quicker and easier to use. By far the most common type, and the one that came to predominate, was the motte-and-bailey.

This type of castle is characterised by a 'motte', a man-made, flat-topped mound of earth and rock, and a 'bailey', a large courtyard at the base of the mound.

The mound was generally enclosed within its own defensive ditch or moat, with a strong timber wall around its summit. The courtyard extended from the foot of the mound, with similar defences comprising a ditch, earth bank and timber wall. Although small castles could on occasion consist of a motte without an attached enclosure, most had one bailey while a few had two or more.

About 1,000 mottes are known in Britain, nearly all built in the first 150 years after the Norman Conquest. The relative speed with which they could be constructed made them a formidable instrument of warfare and conquest.

*Reconstruction by Brian Davison drawn by Ivan Lapper of the courtyard in about 1100. The enclosure would have been crammed with buildings: the lord had a first-floor chamber and chapel. On top of the mound a wooden tower was probably surrounded by a timber palisade*

# DESCRIPTION AND TOUR

❖

## THE CASTLE REMAINS

Totnes Castle is a particularly fine
and well-preserved example of a
large, early Norman motte-and-bailey
castle. The impressive Norman
earthworks were constructed over
900 years ago, almost certainly by
Juhel, a commander in William the
Conqueror's army, soon after the
Normans swept through the South-
West in 1068.

Originally, the courtyard would
have been crowded with wooden
buildings. Both the courtyard and
the mound were protected by earth
and timber defences which were later
replaced in stone.

The stone wall (or 'shell keep')
crowning the mound was built in the
early thirteenth century and extensively reconstructed about 100 years
later. At the same time, a new stone
wall was erected around the courtyard at the foot of the mound.

The plan of the castle on the inside
back cover will help you find your way.

## Bailey and curtain wall

When you enter the castle, you step
into the courtyard (or bailey). This
secluded grassed area sheltered by
trees gives little impression now
of how it must have appeared in
Norman times. Then it would have
been bustling with activity and
crammed with timber buildings,
including living quarters, stables,
stores and workshops. The courtyard
provided accommodation for the
lord's household as well as men-at-
arms.

It was placed on the side of the
castle away from the town to avoid
demolishing too much valuable
commercial property in the town.
An earth bank originally enclosed the
courtyard and would have been
faced by a strong timber fence in
much the same position as the
present stone wall. The stone wall is
largely recent, although its thicker
parts are medieval in date.

We know that by the later medieval
period, at least one fine stone building

*The ditch on the northern side of the courtyard*

*Building a castle mound: a scene from the Bayeux Tapestry*

From the mid-fourteenth century Totnes Castle ceased to be the chief residence of its owners, and by the early fifteenth century we hear of a constable being appointed to run affairs on their behalf. In 1538, it was said that the domestic lodgings were 'clean in ruin', although the castle wall and keep were still maintained.

## Defensive ditches and banks

It is worth walking out through the small gateway opposite the entrance to the castle to view the impressive earthwork defences surrounding the courtyard. Here there is a large, steep-sided ditch, originally flanked by a strong outer bank. Beyond this, there are traces of another, outer courtyard and ditch which appears to have reinforced the defences on this side, possibly enclosing a secure

stood in the courtyard, since excavations revealed ornamental limestone imported from Purbeck in Dorset – 'Purbeck marble' – as well as roofing slates and glazed roofing tiles.

This was probably part of the residence of the medieval lords of the castle which would have included at least a hall with kitchens and a chapel.

MICHAEL HOLFORD

area for holding horses and livestock. These defences protected the main entrance to the Norman castle, which was sited on the side of the courtyard opposite the mound, as commonly found elsewhere. We can imagine timber bridges crossing the ditches, with perhaps a drawbridge lowered from the main gate.

Originally, a ditch around the mound would have separated it from the courtyard. There would then have been another timber bridge crossing it leading up to the summit of the mound, or to a steep flight of wooden steps rising straight to the top.

## Mound and tower

Climbing the modern steps up the mound, the immense scale of the Norman earthworks becomes apparent. The mound is one of the largest in the country. It was built up in layers of pounded earth and rubble, probably using forced Saxon labour. It stands within the circuit of the Saxon town defences, which were clearly breached at this point, and on ground where there had probably been Saxon houses.

The mound was intended to over-awe the townspeople and keep a watchful eye on them. Even today, you can look out across the rooftops of Totnes town from its top. When newly built, it must have been even more impressive. It also provided a last bastion of refuge should the courtyard defences be overrun.

Standing inside the keep, you can see at ground level some stone foundations marking the position of a rectangular tower. Excavation showed that the foundations continue down beyond a depth of 3.4m (11ft), probably to natural rock, and were

MICHAEL HOLFORD

*This scene from the Bayeux Tapestry, showing the attack on Dinan in Brittany, illustrates how the castle's mound and its wooden tower would have been used as a fighting platform of last resort. It also shows how vulnerable timber-walled castles were to attack by fire.*

*The entrance to the keep*

*Interior of keep with the stone foundations of the Norman timber tower in the foreground*

built as part of the Norman construction. The foundations are on average only 0.76m (2ft 6in) wide, which seems too narrow to support a tall tower of stone, so above ground level the tower was probably built of wood. This tower formed the innermost stronghold, and must have contained a number of floors rising high above the castle defences.

Most Norman mottes had such towers built on them, and it is thought that these were initially occupied by the lord himself. This may possibly have been the case at Totnes, but it is difficult to imagine Juhel residing very long in such cramped conditions – each room in the tower measured only 4m by 4.9m (13ft by 16ft) at most. It seems likely that he would have erected a more spacious and comfortable house in the courtyard as soon as it was safe to do so. Other

possible uses for the tower include a watchtower, guardrooms, and space for storing valuables, military equipment and emergency provisions. Its uppermost floor might also have been intended for use as a fighting platform, like some of the towers shown in the Bayeux Tapestry. Part of the tower, if not all, was demolished sometime before the early thirteenth century.

The summit of the mound would originally have been ringed by its own timber wall. Inside, there were few, if any buildings other than the tower until about 1200, when the mound was occupied for a short period, perhaps as temporary military quarters. Excavations uncovered traces of a rather modest domestic structure of this date to the southwest of the tower, with rubble footings for cob or timber walls and a hearth for cooking.

## Stone keep

The stone keep was probably built to replace the Norman timber structure at the beginning of the fourteenth century, or perhaps a little earlier. All trace of any earlier masonry was removed. This date of construction (or reconstruction) is surprisingly late by comparison with other 'shell' keeps of this type in England which generally belong to the late twelfth century.

The keep is nearly circular and measures on average 21m (70ft) in internal diameter. It is the largest and

best preserved of the three such keeps in Devon (those at Plympton and Barnstaple are now mere stumps). It is similar in style to the well-preserved keeps at Launceston, Trematon and Restormel in Cornwall, although these all had spacious accommodation provided within them, whereas the keep at Totnes evidently only ever had a single, lean-to building, erected against its inside. This stood between the entrance and a garderobe or latrine built into the thickness of the shell keep wall. The garderobe was lit by two cross loops (arrow slits), one subsequently made into a larger window. The lean-to has long since disappeared, leaving behind only six projecting corbel stones which once supported its roof, and the stub of a radial wall that supported one of its sides.

The walls of the keep are built of local limestone rubble, with dressings of red sandstone from the Torbay area. The entrance arch, consisting

*Reconstruction by Brian Davison drawn by Ivan Lapper showing the castle being rebuilt in stone in the fourteenth century. Such major building projects were expensive, and required considerable labour. Specialist craftsmen would have been involved in cutting and preparing the stone*

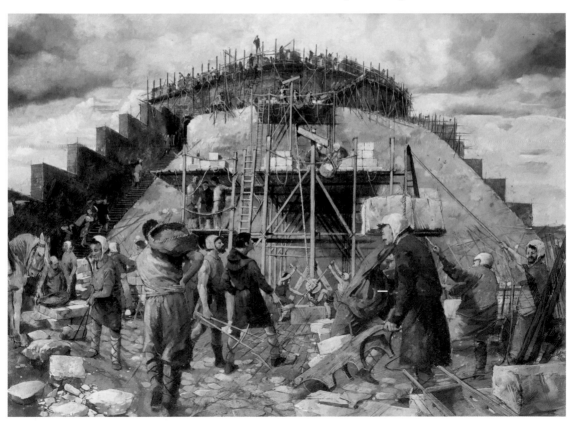

of a double ring of chamfered sandstone blocks, was narrowed in the later medieval period, when its eastern side was rebuilt with dressed sandstone robbed from elsewhere in the building. Inside, close to the keep entrance, two stairways rise to the parapet, which retains remarkably complete battlements.

The battlements are made up of the raised parts (merlons), separated by gaps (crenels). For most of the circuit, broad merlons pierced by arrow slits alternate with narrow unpierced ones, although on the west and north, they are all of the same width and all pierced. Some of the slits are plain while others have a cross slit for sighting, sometimes cut into a sandstone jamb.

These differences in the arrangement and detail of the merlons suggest that some parts of the battlements were repaired in the later medieval period, as does the rough workmanship of many of the merlons around the southern and western sides (the sides overlooking the town).

Beside the keep entrance, the wall straightens for a short distance to provide better cover in front of the entrance way from arrow slits which face in this one direction. Nearby is a large merlon with two arrow slits, one facing north, the other east. The adjacent merlon to the east is also large and has two arrow slits. These reinforced the entrance against a flanking attack.

# THE CASTLE IN RUINS

In about 1538 the Tudor traveller and writer John Leland visited Totnes and noted that 'the castle wall and strong dungeon [keep] be maintained', but that the 'lodgings of the castle be clean in ruin'. There were episodes before this when the castle had been neglected and fallen into disrepair, doubtless because many of its later medieval lords had interests elsewhere, and frequently left the castle in the care of a constable. Even as early as 1273, it was said to contain certain buildings in poor condition, including the hall, chamber and chapel, as well as partly broken down walls on the mound. In 1326, the king commanded that the castle and its fortifications be made good. In 1463, and again in 1471, certain tenants of the lord were compelled to repair the battlements of the castle, while little or nothing was done to the residential buildings in the courtyard. In 1466, a local man was summoned for felling trees growing on the castle ditch, suggesting that the earthwork defences were not maintained, and had become overgrown.

By the sixteenth century, if not before, the castle looked much as it does today. The historian Lysons states that it was reoccupied during the Civil War, but that it was gutted in 1645 on the approach of the Parliamentary commander, Sir Thomas Fairfax, towards Dartmouth.

In 1764, the ruined castle was bought by the Duke of Somerset, whose family, the Seymours of nearby Berry Pomeroy Castle, had owned it temporarily once before. Successors of the duke planted the trees in the bailey, which are between 130 and 175 years old. In the 1920s and 30s the castle was opened to the public for cream teas and a tennis court occupied the flattened area at the centre of the courtyard until the 1950s. During the Second World War evacuees camped in the castle.

The granite pillars that presently stand to either side of the castle entrance come from the old Fruit Market House which was built in 1616 next to parish church. Other pillars from this building now form part of the loggia built in 1897 in front of the sixteenth-century Guildhall. In 1947 the Duke of Somerset placed the castle in the guardianship of the Ministry of Works. Since 1984 it has been in the care of English Heritage.

Archaeological excavations were carried out at Totnes Castle in 1950–53 by Stuart Rigold to discover more about the castle. The interior of the keep was excavated, and investigations made about the remains of buildings in the courtyard.

*Nineteenth-century engraving of Totnes Castle, from Cotton's Sketches of the Antiquities of Totnes*

# HISTORY OF THE CASTLE AND TOWN

❖

THE NAME TOTNES probably comes from the Saxon words 'Tot', meaning lookout, and 'Ness' meaning a low promontory or nose of land. The town stands on an ancient ridgeway which crossed the River Dart at its lowest fordable point. The present walled town has origins dating back more than 1,000 years. It was founded in the first half of the tenth century as one of four royal fortified towns or 'burhs' in Devon, the others being Exeter, Barnstaple and Lydford.

Burhs were defended strongholds constructed during the troubled times of late Saxon England mainly against attack by Vikings. They not only provided refuge for the local Saxon population, but also served as forts capable of accommodating a garrison of soldiers.

In the late ninth and early tenth centuries, King Alfred and his son Edward the Elder established a network of these towns throughout their kingdom of Wessex, which stretched across most of southern and midland England. They were sited at strategic positions such as the meeting of roads, river crossings, the head of estuaries and river mouth sites, each being maintained and garrisoned by men from the surrounding area.

This helped secure the country-side and counter Viking seaborne raids. With such protection in place, the kings of Wessex were free to manoeuvre their best fighting forces with greater mobility, and to campaign for longer periods in the field. Alfred's successors were thus able to reconquer Danish-held territories in the north and east of England, making them kings of all England.

Where the burh towns had Roman walls, such as Exeter, these were reused and made good. Where none such existed, new forts were laid out with earth ramparts and walls of timber or stone. Some were occupied only in times of threat, while others attracted permanent populations, particularly those sited in favourable positions for trade, which benefited from the security and stability they offered.

Trade encouraged growth, and many such settlements later developed into successful, prosperous towns with their own market, crafts, industries and a mint issuing coins. These were among the first truly urban centres in England since Roman times. Many of them survive as thriving towns today.

### The later Saxon town

For 100 years Saxon Totnes prospered. It was the only port on the Dart estuary at this time (Dartmouth only developed from the twelfth century) and it was probably involved from an early date in the export of tin brought down from Dartmoor. Its government remained in royal hands, although by 1018 it had its own 'Witan', or court of wise men. The Witan can be regarded as the forerunner of the later borough council.

Totnes probably suffered from raids in the years around 1000 when the South-West, like many other parts of England, was harried and plundered by Danish raiders. Most

*A silver penny of the Saxon King Aethelred II (978–1016), minted at Totnes by the moneyer Wulfmaer (Totnes Town Council)*

*Location plan of Totnes and the surrounding area*

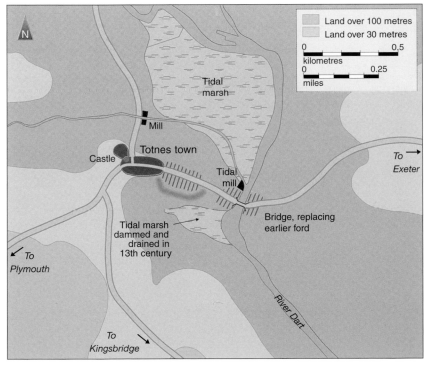

Land over 100 metres
Land over 30 metres

0             0,5
kilometres
0        0.25
miles

N

Tidal marsh

Mill

Totnes town

Castle

Tidal mill

To Exeter

Tidal marsh dammed and drained in 13th century

Bridge, replacing earlier ford

To Plymouth

River Dart

To Kingsbridge

of the surviving coins from the Saxon Totnes mint have been found in Scandinavia, probably paid as tribute, or 'Danegeld'. Some towns with timber defences were refortified in stone at this period, so the origins of the present stone town wall at Totnes may lie in this period.

## The Normans arrive

William the Conqueror's Norman army swept through the South-West between December 1067 and March 1068. They came to crush a Saxon uprising in the region, led by the men of Exeter. William forced Exeter to surrender following a siege of 18 days, then continued his campaign through the remainder of Devon and Cornwall. We hear of no further resistance, so it seems likely that Totnes had little choice but to submit and bow to Norman authority. Totnes was already an important trading town with access to the sea and a relatively large population.

*Reconstruction drawing by Ivan Lapper of Totnes in Norman times. The timber-walled castle has been imposed upon the layout of the Saxon town, while a new settlement outside the walls stretches towards the River Dart crossing*

William must have looked on it both as a potential centre for further Saxon revolt, and as a valuable prize.

## Juhel of Totnes and the castle

There is no written record to tell us who built the castle at Totnes, or precisely when, but there can be little doubt that it was Juhel, or Judhael, a commander in William's south-western campaign, who was probably a Breton rather than a true Norman.

Juhel does not seem to have fought at the Battle of Hastings in 1066, so probably joined William when he turned his attention to the South-West. For his service, Juhel was rewarded by William with the grant of Totnes and over 100 manors concentrated in South Devon. Juhel is recorded as holding these properties in the great Domesday survey of England made for William the Conqueror in 1086, by which time he had settled here and become known as Juhel of Totnes.

*Reconstruction drawing by Ivan Lapper of Totnes in the fourteenth century. By this time the castle had been rebuilt in stone, the town had grown, the Dart had been bridged, and a tidal inlet in the river had been drained to form farmland*

*Finds from medieval Totnes:
an ivory chess piece (top);
a piece of carved bone
(middle); part of an iron
horse bridle (bottom)
(Totnes Museum)*

The Domesday survey tells us that the borough of Totnes was worth £3 before the Norman Conquest. This had risen to £8 by 1086, making it the second largest and wealthiest town in Devon after Exeter. The increase in value probably reflects the overall increase in the wealth and number of townspeople, whose number at this time is recorded as 95 'burgesses', or heads of households, plus 15 more outside the borough who worked the land. The total population, taking families into account, would have numbered about 500 people.

Juhel also founded and endowed a priory within the walls of the town. The priory church, dedicated to St Mary, stood close to the site of the present fifteenth-century parish church, and probably replaced a Saxon church in much the same position. The priory cloister lay between the church and the town wall to its north, and would have had buildings arranged around it, the ones adjacent to the town wall standing approximately on the site of the present Guildhall.

Juhel appears to have fallen from royal favour at the time of death of William I. He may have supported the rebellion of 1088 against William II, and consequently been driven into exile. He certainly forfeited his English estates, and we hear no more of him for ten years or so.

In 1089, Totnes and other of Juhel's properties were granted by William II to one of his favourites, Roger de Nonant, whose family thereafter held the town and castle for three more generations.

Juhel's fortunes revived under Henry I when he returned to Devon and was compensated for the loss of Totnes with the borough and manor of Barnstaple, where he built another castle and priory. He died at a great age in about 1123.

## The castle in the Middle Ages

Roger de Nonant was a close companion of the king, and spent most of his time away from Totnes. He appointed a steward to collect the revenues from his Totnes estates, as did his descendants. The Nonants held Totnes and its castle until 1205, when King John granted the majority of the estate to William de Braose, who claimed descent from Juhel through the female line.

William de Braose himself fell from favour about three years later, and Totnes was given to Henry, son of the Earl of Cornwall, an illegitimate son of Henry I. But in 1219, when Henry's estates were in turn confiscated, Totnes was returned to the Braose family. It may have been Reginald, son of William de Braose, who built the first stone keep on the mound and some fine stone buildings in the courtyard.

Through Reginald's sister Eva, the castle passed to her husband,

William de Cantelupe, whose family was prominent in the borderlands of Wales. In 1244, during William's lordship, we first hear of the tenants' (William's vassals) duty to maintain and garrison the castle whenever required. Tenants holding property assessed at 28 'knight's fees' were expected to provide one man-at-arms for each fee, and every two fees were to be responsible for repairing three crenellations of the castle keep. It seems, however, that the Cantelupes took little interest in the castle as a residence, for in 1273 we hear of extensive dilapidation.

Such neglect continued under the de la Zouche family to whom Totnes passed by marriage sometime after 1286. The Zouches were a powerful family whose main estates lay in Northamptonshire. It was in the time of William de la Zouche, in 1326, that a royal order came to refortify the castle. The order may merely have sanctioned work already undertaken on rebuilding the keep, which is thought to have been built sometime around this time. The Zouches continued enforcing maintenance of the keep on their tenants, but evidently did little to the residential buildings and courtyard wall. They assigned a constable to manage the affairs of the castle on their behalf. The constable held a manorial court at the castle, but little else happened there.

The situation was much the same in 1485 when Totnes and the castle passed from the Zouches, who supported the Yorkists in the War of the Roses, to the Lancastrian Sir Richard Edgecombe of Cotehele. From then on, the castle ceased to be used either as a fortification or residence, and thereafter deteriorated rapidly.

Throughout its entire Norman and medieval history, there is no record of the castle ever having being involved in military action. Its main role was as a centre for local administration and justice. From an early date a steward or constable was in charge and carried out the lord's duties in his absence.

*Engraving of the town's North Gate, 1810*

*The ramparts walk leading to the Guildhall*

*The town's East Gate*

## THE TOWN

Totnes borough experienced changing fortunes in the medieval period. In Juhel's time, it ranked second among the towns of Devon. There would already have been a weekly market attracting local business, and for a brief spell around 1100, the Totnes mint started issuing coins following a lapse of about 80 years. In 1131, the town obtained the grant of an annual fair, which appears to have lasted 11 days from the 1st of May, and which would have attracted many more buyers and traders from considerable distances.

The townspeople busied themselves in shipbuilding, fishing, tanning hides, leatherwork, and making woollen cloth. Apart from tin, the town exported large quantities of roofing slates from quarries nearby, including, in 1180, 800,000 slates for Winchester Castle. By the end of the twelfth century, if not before, it is likely that the built-up area had extended down the hill from East Gate to a quay on the River Dart. Totnes bridge was standing by the early thirteenth century, when Bridgetown Pomeroy, a rival borough on the opposite bank of the Dart, was established. The town wall certainly existed by 1205, and was repaired in 1265, and again in 1313. The town continued to be commercially active throughout medieval times, although its position in the ranking of Devon towns was overtaken by other, newer towns such as Dartmouth and Plymouth which had grown up closer to the sea as deepwater ports.

Totnes rose to prominence again between the fifteenth century and mid-seventeenth century, a period of great prosperity for the town, due largely to the booming trade in woollen cloth, which benefited many parts of Devon at this time. The town's merchants dominated the overseas trade of the port of Dartmouth, exporting cloth and tin to France in return for linen and manufactured goods. In 1524–25, Totnes was four times as wealthy as Dartmouth, and ranked sixteenth out of all the provincial towns in England.

In the mid-fifteenth century, the aspiring parishioners used their wealth to rebuild the church of St Mary, which has an unusually elaborate tower and one of the most perfect stone screens in England.

When the church was built, the old priory founded by Juhel was still standing on adjoining ground. The end of the priory came in 1536, at the beginning of the Dissolution of the Monasteries under Henry VIII. The priory buildings were stripped of all valuable materials and completely dismantled, apart from one corner of the priory church which was left standing to buttress the chancel of the new parish church. The remains of the junction between the two churches can be seen at the east end of the present church. The land where the priory buildings had stood was eventually passed to the town council, who built the present Guildhall on the site.

During the sixteenth and seventeenth century, the merchants of Totnes rebuilt almost all the town houses on major street frontages, thereby creating one of the finest collections of such buildings to survive anywhere in the country. From the 1570s to the early 1600s, the population expanded from an estimated 1,700 to about 2,500. The town had three annual fairs by this time, and several specialised markets, for cattle, meat, fish, fruit and vegetables, corn, wool, yarn and cloth. But by 1600, the trade in Dartmoor tin had all but dried up, and the town's export of cloth was rapidly falling. From the 1640s onwards, a marked decline set in. In 1719, the town council was declared insolvent, and disposed of nearly all its property on long leases in order to raise money.

Thereafter the town settled into the routines of a small market town, remaining largely undisturbed by the arrival of the railway in 1848.

*'A prospect of Totnes', by William Tomkins (1730–92)*

# ❖ THE LEGACY OF SAXON AND NORMAN TIMES ❖

Remarkably, Totnes has remained largely unspoilt. Most modern development has taken place outside the town walls and many features of the Saxon town layout are still preserved and visible today, seen to best advantage either on the town plan or from the air. The oval shape traced by the Saxon defences can be picked out by the back streets and alleys which grew up alongside the town wall. The single main street – High Street – is Saxon in origin. So too, probably, is the broadening of the street in the area now flanked by the Butterwalk and Poultry Walk, indicating the site of an early market place. The present East Gate stands on the site of one of two Saxon gateways which must have led out through the town defences at either end of High Street. The regular pattern of long thin property holdings, stretching back from the main street to the town wall, was almost certainly first laid out in Saxon times.

The Norman castle was clearly imposed on this existing Saxon layout, since it interrupts and lies astride the line of the earlier defences. Its tall mound and keep stand inside the town, while its courtyard was laid out on open ground outside the town defences. Castle Street grew up next to the castle ditch, leading from the market place in High Street to the North Gate beside the castle entrance, which still retains its plain, round archway dating probably from the twelfth century.

We seldom see such a clear picture of a town's early history, especially one founded in Saxon times, still preserved today – something which makes the town of Totnes such an important link with the past.

*Totnes from the air. Features such as the castle, parish church, and the oval shape of the Saxon town defences can clearly be seen*

STEWART BROWN